W9-CIP-870

STEEPLE CHASE

Jeff Hagen

Pfeifer-Hamilton Publishers
Duluth, Minnesota

Pfeifer-Hamilton Publishers
210 West Michigan
Duluth, MN 55802-1908   218-727-0500

Steeple Chase

©1997 by Jeff Hagen. All rights reserved. Except for short excerpts for review purposes, no part of this book may be reproduced or transmitted in any form by any means, electronic or mechanical, including photocopying, without permission in writing from the publisher.

Printed in the Republic of Korea by Doosan Dong-A Co. Ltd.

10   9   8   7   6   5   4   3   2   1

Editorial Director: Susan Gustafson

Art Director: Joy Morgan Dey

Library of Congress Catalog Card Number: 96-60663

ISBN 1-57025-130-4

To my son Kit

TRAVELING MISSION ROAD

I grew up on Mission Road, a mile-long dusty lane that meanders through oak and juniper trees just south of Minneapolis. It lies near the old Shakopee trail where a pioneer missionary named Gideon Pond once preached to Dakota Indians who lived among the bluffs and hollows of the Minnesota River valley.

In a sense, I'm still on Mission Road.

During the past twelve years, I have sought out and worshipped in more than 150 rural chapels, churches, and cathedrals, following a path that wanders deep into the valley of time.

Many of the proud edifices I've visited still have living, active congregations. Others, adorned in the patina of time, wearing weathered coats of faded gray, rest abandoned on desolate rural roads. They appeared lifeless, but as I looked more closely and listened, I could almost hear distant echoes of laughter and tears, stirring sermons, and joyful weddings, sorrowful funerals, and jubilant church picnics of Sundays past.

On my journey, I learned more about my own faith by experiencing that of others. I learned about strong core values that are still practiced in these small places. I felt refreshed as I paused in the warmth of each small group of worshippers, living their commitment to God, family, neighbors, and friends in a corner of the world they inherited from their ancestors. From these churches, I learned about devoted loyalty and persistence, about life and death and love, about stability amidst change. In these churches, I rediscovered a valuable part of my own soul and a renewal of my faith.

BATHTUB MADONNA

My steeple chase was not frantic or hurried as the words might suggest. It was leisurely, pursued over several years. During those years, time has already changed many of the churches I sketched. You will also find that my drawings of these churches are not architecturally accurate depictions. They reflect what I felt as much as what I saw. The images I've created are renderings of my soul on the landscape of my heart.

In the pages of this book, I invite you to join me on my journey. Let it touch you and call out memories from your own personal history. Through these reflections, I hope that you, too, can journey to the heartland of your spirit.

Jeff Hagen
1996

ACKNOWLEDGMENTS

I thank the Wisconsin Historical Society and the Minnesota Division of Tourism for their assistance. Special gratitude to Shirley Raymaker, Maria Moeller, and Allen Pease. Thanks also to Bill Nelson, Beth Slocum, Alan Borsuch, and Carol Guensburg, who provided great help and support when they shared the journalistic helm at the *Milwaukee Journal Sunday Magazine,* and to Brian Howell at the *Wisconsin State Journal.*

I am especially grateful to all the people who took the time to jot down their personal affirmations and reflections on what going to church means to them. Special thanks to pastors Bill Redman and Jonathon Rice for the support and infinite wisdom they brought to this endeavor and to all the people at Pfeifer-Hamilton for their faith and undying patience.

CHIPPEWA MISSION,
CHIPPEWA VALLEY, WISCONSIN

SPRING

In the warm spring sunshine, plow blades cut deep into fields, turning over the rich black loam once sought by immigrant farmers. European soils, depleted by centuries of farming and divided into tiny plots, could no longer support extended families. Young men and women left their homelands seeking the vast prairies of America's heartland.

Before they left their homes and families, they prayed for guidance. They prayed for courage during their difficult journey and for endurance as they struggled to turn deep-rooted prairie sod into fields of wheat and corn. Then, in thanksgiving to the God who brought them safely to this new land, they built houses of prayer.

*T*he first buildings erected by settlers provided shelter for their families, but soon after they completed these humble homes for their bodies, they began building homes for their souls. Although they had little time or money to spare, the churches they built were always far more beautiful than their simple houses.

The steeple of Cross of Christ Lutheran Church, which sits on a rise of land just north of Red Wing, Minnesota, can be seen for miles. In early times, local farmers looked toward that hill for inspiration and encouragement. Cross of Christ's steeple was the center of their world—a safe harbor for spirit and soul. For many, it still is.

CROSS OF CHRIST LUTHERAN CHURCH, RED WING, MINNESOTA

*M*ore than two hundred years ago, black-robed Jesuits left their cloistered seminaries to paddle and portage northern lakes and trails along with the voyageurs. Their goal was to share their faith with the native peoples of this new land.

In 1731, Father Charles Measaiger blazed the trail to Grand Portage, Minnesota. He was followed by many other missionaries, but the first cedar-bark and deer-skin chapel was not built until a hundred years later. Our Lady of the Holy Rosary, a log church, was erected in 1865 and to this day continues to serve both Native Americans and the descendants of immigrant Americans.

OUR LADY OF THE HOLY ROSARY CATHOLIC CHURCH, GRAND PORTAGE, MINNESOTA

*C*yclists who pedal the Military Ridge Trail in southern Wisconsin pass near the Simpson Chapel. It looks more like a cottage than a church, but for eighty years, a small Methodist congregation worshipped within its walls. The little frame building was constructed elsewhere, towed to this site by a team of oxen, then placed on its stone foundation. To people without a church, it was welcomed like a cathedral. Now it remains a monument to the simplicity of those bygone days.

SIMPSON CHAPEL, DODGEVILLE, WISCONSIN

*T*owering bluffs and rocky outcroppings surround Immanuel Lutheran Church, built by German immigrants in the coulee country of eastern Minnesota. Through the deep valleys of this rough, hilly area, frigid streams rush down to the Mississippi River.

In the midst of this difficult land, the immigrants discovered a peaceful glen with fertile land for farming. With hopeful hearts, they called it Flower Valley. Midway down the valley they built their church, complete with tongue and groove oak interior and a chandelier suspended from the chapel ceiling. Beautiful, solid, the proud little church resonates peace and sincerity in this lush valley nestled deep in a protected fold of God's country.

IMMANUEL LUTHERAN CHURCH, HAY CREEK, MINNESOTA 11

*B*ats in the belfry, mice in the cellar, skunks under the back porch—some of the tales may be apocryphal, but they're part of the folklore that surrounds each church. And there are other stories.

First Presbyterian Church in Pardeeville, Wisconsin, was only partially constructed when the Civil War began. The construction was stopped because all the men went off to war—well, all except one. As the story goes, to avoid military service, one man hid in the newly built steeple, emerging only at night to find food. Whether factual or fanciful, stories like this give each church its own special character.

FIRST PRESBYTERIAN CHURCH, PARDEEVILLE, WISCONSIN

*W*e marvel at the difficulty of building Egyptian pyramids, constructed of stone by human hands alone. It wasn't much easier to build the Congregational Church in Shopiere, Wisconsin. The stone was cut with chisel and mallet from a church member's quarry and was hauled on carts to the building site. Shovels, not bulldozers, excavated the foundation. Heavy stones were lifted into place by people, not cranes. Mortar was mixed by hand. Holes were drilled with brace and bit. And all the work was accomplished by members whose skills had been honed as they built their own homes and barns. The work was done precisely; it was done beautifully; it was done to the glory of God—a testimony of labor that still stands as a witness to faith.

SHOPIERE CONGREGATIONAL CHURCH, SHOPIERE, WISCONSIN

*M*any thriving towns of a century ago were abandoned when the railroad era ended. Ironically, although those little towns have disappeared from the prairie, their churches often remain. Some still draw worshippers from surrounding farms. Others, like Valley Grove Church near Nerstrand, Minnesota, have become historic preservation sites.

Valley Grove Church, once a center of activity for the farm families who worked the fields and lived in the valley beneath it, now stands as a monument to the pioneers who built it.

The church, perched high on a hill above swaying fields of corn, faces the sunrise. People gather in this parklike setting for weddings and other special events, welcoming the future as they celebrate the past.

VALLEY GROVE CHURCH, NEAR NERSTRAND, MINNESOTA 17

A passerby would never guess that Island Church has not had an active congregation for more than one hundred years. From 1863 to 1891, it served families who had emigrated from four Bohemian villages within walking distance of each other. At that time, it was called St. Wenceslaus Catholic Church in honor of the patron saint of Bohemia.

As the years went by, it became impractical to provide a priest for the tiny mission. So it was the members, who by then were worshipping in nearby Waterloo, who took care of the 750-square-foot tamarack-log building, protecting it from vandalism and decay for nearly a century. It is now maintained by a nonprofit foundation, still supported financially, in part, by descendants of the original members.

ST. WENCESLAUS ISLAND CHURCH, WATERLOO, WISCONSIN

*T*he words "St. Johns Evan. Luth. Church" carved above the door of Lakeview Lutheran Chapel in Madison, Wisconsin, reflect the mergers and name changes that are part of this church's history.

But the stories people remember are its greatest heritage: the custodians who served for more than fifty years, paid at first with only the pennies received in the offering; an Easter morning when the pastor's horse, sunk to its belly in mud, was dragged out in time for the pastor to arrive at the sunrise service; and the faithful people who persevered during good times and bad.

Churches facing budgetary woes today might find Lakeview's 1884 budget quite intriguing: annual income $12.88, expenses $12.08.

LAKEVIEW LUTHERAN CHAPEL, MADISON, WISCONSIN

*T*he beautiful churches pioneers built with care would have tumbled to the ground within just a few decades had their descendants not continued to provide loving maintenance and care. Week after week, in sunshine, rain, and snow, members rose early on Sundays to light fires in potbellied wood stoves. They painted clapboard siding, cut grass, and raked leaves. They served suppers that paid for shingles and spent several long Saturdays every few years repairing the roof.

Members of one family willingly provided that kind of loving care for their church in Herbster, Wisconsin.

My mother and sisters dusted and cleaned the church. Dad built fires and shoveled snow for years. We are part of this church, we refuse to let it die.

—DOROTHY BURKLAND

HERBSTER COMMUNITY CHURCH, HERBSTER, WISCONSIN

I visited this Congregational Church in Spring Green one Sunday morning when I was struggling with grief and healing from a major personal loss. The community welcomed me unconditionally and provided the warmth that I needed on a day when the road of life seemed harsh and cruel. —J.H.

SPRING GREEN CONGREGATIONAL CHURCH, SPRING GREEN, WISCONSIN 25

A well-tended cemetery borders St. Paul Lutheran Church in Marxville, Wisconsin. On Memorial Day, when the community commemorates those who fought and died to preserve their freedom, the churchyard is alive with flags and flowers.

On this day, in churches throughout America, people recall their loved ones and pray fervently for peace and for the safety of those who defend it.

> *Eternal Father, strong to save,*
> *Whose arm has bound the restless wave,*
> *Who bade the might ocean deep*
> *Its own appointed limits keep;*
> *O, hear us when we cry to thee*
> *For those in peril on the sea.*

ST. PAUL LUTHERAN CHURCH, MARXVILLE, WISCONSIN

OUR LADY OF THE FIELDS CHURCH
PLAIN, WISCONSIN

SUMMER

Brilliant blue skies shimmered over acres of green prairie ablaze with wild flowers. Farmers gazed with pride at lush fields of corn, oats, and wheat. Summer had arrived in the heartland and with it the abundant crops sought by pioneers. These hardy farm families survived the winter blizzards that killed their livestock, and they replanted their crops after spring floods washed away their seeds.

From bitter experience, they knew that even bountiful crops could be destroyed in a few moments by hail, tornado, or wildfire. And if the rains refused to fall, the plants would quickly scorch in the summer sun. So, throughout the summer, they watched and waited and continued to pray. They prayed for simple things: the blessings of good crops and healthy children. And they prayed that God would make them worthy of the blessings they sought.

At one time, a church stood at the very heart of each rural community. It provided space for the town's social and cultural activities as well as its religious life. Children stumbled through recitals on the church's piano; community choruses sang in its balcony; citizens cast their ballots in the basement; and on the Fourth of July, patriotic speeches rang out on the church lawn.

Longtime members of Buena Vista Church remember wonderful picnics on hot summer days that were cooled by hand-churned ice cream. They recall the delight of childhood games, the joy of teenage romances blossoming slowly under the watchful eyes of older church members, and the pure pleasure enjoyed by adults who, for this one day, could rest from their labors.

BUENA VISTA UNITED METHODIST CHURCH, PLOVER, WISCONSIN

During the eighteenth and nineteenth centuries, many country churches were served by circuit riding preachers who visited each parish perhaps once a month. Traveling on horseback from one tiny congregation to another, they paused in each community just long enough to lead services, baptize infants, marry couples, and teach the basics of Bible and doctrine to young people.

Sharing a pastor with other communities made it possible for congregations to form even though they could not afford a fulltime staff. It's not so different today. Churches like North Windsor United Methodist continue to exist because they share their pastor with other congregations. This can be difficult for both the pastor and the members, but their spirit of cooperation makes it possible for small congregations to survive.

NORTH WINDSOR UNITED METHODIST CHURCH, DEFOREST, WISCONSIN

*W*hen you stroll the lanes of Angel Hill, high above the St. Croix River, you feel a bit closer to heaven than when you walk the busy shopping center of Taylors Falls, Wisconsin. The thirty-eight buildings in this historic district appear to be transplanted from a New England village.

A little fence surrounds the Methodist Church on Angel Hill. It's a replica of the original, which once protected the church-yard from becoming a pasture for sheep and cows that were herded past the church by the town shepherd.

TAYLORS FALLS UNITED METHODIST CHURCH, TAYLORS FALLS, MINNESOTA   35

*M*any rural churches were planned and built by craftsmen who were members of the congregation, but a few were designed by noted architects.

Within sight of Frank Lloyd Wright's Taliesin in Spring Green, Wisconsin, lies a small shingle and limestone chapel dating back to 1886. According to local legend, Frank Lloyd Wright, at age eighteen, designed the church's interior.

UNITY CHAPEL, SPRING GREEN, WISCONSIN

*T*he last time I saw this church on 9½ Street in Barron, Wisconsin, it stood alone and abandoned, gray in the setting sun, its paint faded by harsh winds. At the turn of the century, the church had been dragged more than a mile by work horses to this spot on the edge of the road, the perfect location for its small congregation to gather.

Sadly, the church was recently demolished. Only the steeple is left, now a gazebo on a neighbor's lawn. When passersby notice this remnant, I hope they recall its proud past and offer a prayer of thanksgiving for Sundays of long ago when its church bell rang out, calling townsfolk to worship.

POSKIN METHODIST CHURCH, BARRON, WISCONSIN

*O*n the edge of Lake Superior, St. Francis Xavier Church still stands, the last remaining structure of an Indian village known locally as Chippewa City.

Now the church, founded by Jesuit missionaries and later served by Benedictine fathers, is empty most Sundays. Its former parishioners worship at St. John's Church in Grand Marais. But once every year, on the Fourth of July, members of St. John's gather at the Chippewa Church for worship. In their prayers, they give thanks for the thousands of masses offered in this little church by devoted priests and their equally devoted parishioners.

ST. FRANCIS XAVIER CATHOLIC CHURCH, GRAND MARAIS, MINNESOTA

*G*arrison Keillor tells stories with humor and love about life in his imaginary town, Lake Wobegon—"the town that time forgot." On the edge of Tomorrow River, I discovered Nelsonville, Wisconsin, another town that, like Lake Wobegon, maintains the values of former generations and passes them on to its youth. It may look like progress has passed Nelsonville by, but the people who live there look to the future as well as remember their roots.

With its steeple stretched to the heavens to watch
the sun rise and set, every new day gently and lovingly
reminds me of the marvelous victory
won by light over darkness.

—MARGARET STRATTON

NELSONVILLE LUTHERAN CHURCH, NELSONVILLE, WISCONSIN

*O*nly with great dedication can a church be maintained for more than a century. The members of Castle Rock Church know this. They know that they must care for their building. When I visited this church, I marveled at the polished wood in glowing tones of amber and cinnamon and asked when the rennovations had been made. "We haven't rennovated anything," I was told. "We just maintained and cared for it over the years."

The Castle Rock Church is family to me. I feel related to all members, if not by blood, then by faith and history. These are the people who taught me Bible verses in Sunday School and who taught me what faith is and how to live by their daily example.

—RUTH TOLLEFSON

CASTLE ROCK LUTHERAN CHURCH, CASTLE ROCK, WISCONSIN

*M*embers of Indian Baptist Church welcome visits from the multitude of tourists who throng to Wisconsin Dells each summer.

The church, developed as a mission to the Ho-Chunk Indians, still takes that special calling very seriously. Its Vacation Bible School continues to provide an outreach to the surrounding Native American community.

INDIAN BAPTIST CHURCH, WISCONSIN DELLS, WISCONSIN

Built on a rock the church shall stand,
Even when steeples are falling.

The resounding words of this old hymn proclaim the stability people find in their church, not just in the building but in the faith it represents. Grounded in this faith, they face the turmoil of our modern world with calm courage.

A parishioner reflects on what St. John's Lutheran Church means to her:

This church is more than a rock building. It's
also a rock in the lives of families in our community.

—RHONDA SUTCLIFFE

ST. JOHN'S LUTHERAN CHURCH, MAZOMANIE, WISCONSIN

*O*ut in the country, most funerals aren't held in mortuaries. People are memorialized in the place where they were baptized, confirmed, and married—the place where they worshipped God almost every Sunday throughout their lives.

Cedar Grove Lutheran has been host to many such funerals. And when the service is over, pallbearers, many of whom have performed this labor of love dozens of times, struggle down the front steps carrying their heavy load. When their friend is finally laid to rest in the earth, they return to the church to eat, to console each other, and to celebrate the life of their loved one.

CEDAR GROVE LUTHERAN CHURCH, PICKWICK, MINNESOTA

*I*n the summer of 1876, Rocky Mountain grasshoppers—first thousands, then millions—invaded Minnesota, devouring everything in their path and leaving devastation behind. After eating crops down to the ground, they laid their eggs in the earth to await the next spring. Farmers, too, helplessly, waited for spring, trying to summon the courage to risk their savings and plant once again.

In response to this plague, Father Leo Winter felt moved to build a chapel dedicated to the Blessed Mother, a place for repentance and prayer. Assumption Chapel was constructed and dedicated the following year. The people prayed for deliverance, and the grasshoppers disappeared.

Every Saturday for the next fifteen years, a mass of thanksgiving was offered in what came to be known as Grasshopper Chapel.

ASSUMPTION CHAPEL, COLD SPRING, MINNESOTA

TRIPOLI CONGREGATIONAL CHURCH
TRIPOLI, WISCONSIN

F A L L

Plump ears of corn tumbled into silos; russet potatoes and bright orange squash filled root cellar bins; spotless jars of apples and peaches, green beans and carrots glowed on pantry shelves; pale gold wheat was carted away to provide cash for the few things that couldn't be grown or made at home.

If the year was good and the harvest abundant, the fruits, grains, vegetables, and animal fodder would last throughout the long winter months. But even in years of scarcity, farm families gathered in their churches, bowed their heads in prayer, and sang grateful hymns of praise, giving thanks for the harvest, a gift from God.

*R*eligious education was as important to early settlers as reading, writing, and arithmetic. Children were first taught Bible stories in their own homes, and they were expected to memorize Bible verses. As soon as churches were built, an important duty of pastors was to teach young people the catechism.

Often, religious education took place in church basements, sharing space with Missionary Societies and Ladies Aids, but growing communities and large families soon compelled congregations to add space. Rather than build a larger worship area, they often built an education wing. The large fellowship hall in these additions reflected the growing emphasis on fostering community in an increasingly diverse society.

CHRIST CHURCH, OLD FRONTENAC, MINNESOTA

*O*n the wall of Hauge Church in Perry, Wisconsin, I found this expression of an unknown poet's longing for the simple life this chapel represents.

I sat beside a tiny church
Perched on a valley hill.
I could imagine myself
Sitting here years from now,
My children huddled around me,
My wife holding all our hands in hers.
It would be in evening
In the same kind of autumn
With the winds blowing easier.
The little church will be our home,
And all around would be gardens we had grown.
A simple life is what I ask,
Just a life of hill sitting and west watching.

HAUGE LUTHERAN CHURCH, PERRY, WISCONSIN

*M*any congregations of immigrants continued for years to use the language of their homeland as the language of their worship. In the community of Denzer, Wisconsin, the prayers and sermons were spoken in German.

As the years passed, it became necessary to preach and teach in English if children were to learn the faith, but occasionally services were still held in German. Times continue to change. Now the congregation celebrates World Communion Sunday with services in German, English, and Spanish—thus reaching out to the old and to the young and to the new immigrants.

DENZER UNITED METHODIST CHURCH, DENZER, WISCONSIN   61

*P*eople who remained in Europe during the great emigrations were determined that loved ones who left for America would not forget their faith. To insure this, they sent along priceless religious articles from their churches: Bibles, prayer books, altar missals, crucifixes, chalices, icons, candlesticks, and vestments. Holy Assumption Orthodox Church in Lublin, Wisconsin, still treasures the precious items its Slavic founders brought from Eastern Europe.

HOLY ASSUMPTION ORTHODOX CHURCH, LUBLIN, WISCONSIN 63

$\mathcal{T}$he beautiful, intricately carved woodwork that adorns the altar chapel in Mt. Horeb's Evangelical Lutheran Church is typical of the hand carving found in most Lutheran churches a few decades ago. Many churches also had a painting of Christ in the Garden of Gethsemane, Christ Standing at the Door, or Jesus the Good Shepherd placed above the altar.

Lutherans traveling from one community to another in the heartland could always be sure of finding a church that looked almost like the one at home—a comfort to travelers and a symbol of their shared faith.

EVANGELICAL LUTHERAN CHURCH, MT. HOREB, WISCONSIN

*M*ost churches have a formal name, and sometimes it's quite long. The Catholic church in St. Mary's, Wisconsin, for instance, is Nativity of the Blessed Virgin Mary Roman Catholic Church. Often those churches also have a nickname, and it's that shorter name that everyone in town knows. When the harvest dinner is served each fall, the Baptists, the Methodists, and the Lutherans all feel welcome in St. Mary's Ridge, their friendly hometown Catholic church on the hill.

Overlooking the surrounding farmland, the cross on the steeple of St. Mary's Ridge catches the moonlight, casting a tranquil glow over the farmers who continue their fall plowing into the late evening hours.

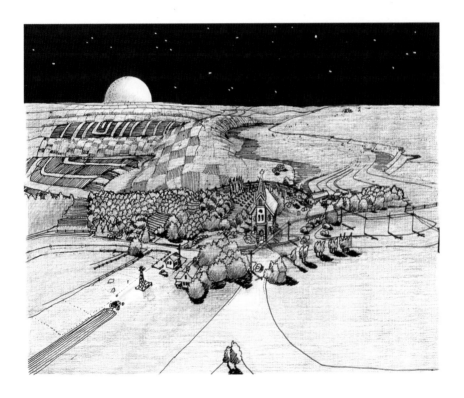

*I*t's overwhelming and humbling to learn that strangers have been praying for you.

The Sunday I was scheduled to visit St. Peter's Lutheran, I slipped on an patch of ice and tumbled to the ground, breaking my arm. The local hospital put a cast on my arm, and I headed out to the church, hoping to get there before the service was over. When I arrived, I found that members of the congregation, who had heard I was injured, had been praying for my safe recovery.

Former strangers now felt like brothers and sisters.

ST. PETER'S LUTHERAN CHURCH, SHENNINGTON, WISCONSIN

$\mathcal{T}$here's a baby here," the elderly man said, "buried in the ditch by the lilac. Sixty years ago, during the great seven-day blizzard, my wife gave birth in our farmhouse here on this land, but our child died. The blizzard was so ferocious we couldn't get any farther than the edge of the road, so we buried our baby right here."

When Justin Isherwood—farmer, author, philosopher— heard this story, he built a memorial to the baby and to the father who came often to stand at the roadside and remember. Justin and his son built a mound of native stones crowned by a tiny sculptured crib—a cradle for this small soul. On the corners of the crib, he welded symbols of Christianity, Islam, Buddhism, and Native American spirituality.

Isherwood, caretaker to the memory of an innocent child, offers good reason for us to reaffirm our faith in humanity.

ISHERWOOD'S CRADLE, STEVENS POINT, WISCONSIN

Come ye thankful people come;
Raise the song of harvest home.
All is safely gathered in
Ere the winter storms begin.
God our maker doth provide
For our wants to be supplied.
Come to God's own temple, come;
Raise the song of harvest home.

All across America, this hymn of praise is sung on Thanksgiving Day, but nowhere more fervently than in churches of the heartland. In churches like Holy Redeemer Catholic in Perry, Wisconsin, people truly know that all good gifts are gifts from God, and for those gifts, they regularly give thanks.

HOLY REDEEMER CATHOLIC CHURCH, PERRY, WISCONSIN

EAST WIOTA LUTHERAN CHURCH
SOUTH WAYNE, WISCONSIN

WINTER

Undeterred by howling blizzards, each week pioneers left their isolated homesteads and trudged miles to experience the hope, the faith, and the sense of community they found in their churches. On a crisp, cold Christmas Eve, as we stroll through softly falling snow towards our own churches, we relive their longing, their commitment, and their joyful anticipation of communion with God and with each other.

We gaze toward the glowing windows; we listen to the strains of *Silent Night* float from the doors as they open to welcome us and our friends and neighbors; and we remember the thousands who entered these doors before us.

A century ago, Russian immigrants traveled from Alaska and California to northern Wisconsin. They came to fish the waters of Lake Superior and to harvest the abundant timber, settling in Cornucopia, a town named for the abundance of fish, apples, and game that surrounded it.

They brought their faith, they brought their Bible, and on a hill overlooking the lake, they built their new spiritual home, St. Mary's Russian Orthodox Church. Atop the onion dome of the small wood frame building stands a cross, the second bar tipped at an angle, signifying the agony that Christ endured.

One hundred years later, the fish and timber era that lured the original settlers has passed into the twilight of history, but the legacy, the spirit, and the religious freedom harvested by those Russian immigrants is still in abundant supply.

ST. MARY'S RUSSIAN ORTHODOX CHURCH, CORNUCOPIA, WISCONSIN　77

*M*ore than a century after they were founded, many rural churches still retain their ethnic roots. The Lutheran Church in Vasa, Minnesota, built by Swedish immigrants, and named for King Gustav Vasa, is one such church.

But even in "the most Swedish colony in America" changes occur. The day I visited, organ music reverberated throughout the church and into the parking lot that held only a single pickup truck. But the musician didn't look a bit Swedish. A man wearing a cowboy hat was playing the organ— playing it very well. The sole occupant of the church, he seemed surprised and a little chagrined to have company. I asked him if he was the church's music director. "Nope," he replied, "I grew up around here many years ago. Whenever I come back to visit, I come in here to play. It's my peace; it's my passion."

VASA LUTHERAN CHURCH, VASA, MINNESOTA

*R*ivers were the pathways along which many settlers traveled to their new homes, and communities often were built on their banks. Perched high above the Mississippi River, Homer United Methodist Church has for years stood watch over steamboats and freight trains in the valley below. The tiny community of Homer was founded by Willard Bunnell, who chose this spot on the river because it had good pasture land and fewer rattle-snakes than another landing across the river.

In 1901, the original church was struck by lightning. A member ran into the burning church and dragged out the altar chairs and pulpit, saving them from the fire. They became the heart of the new church, constructed on the old foundation. Today this little sanctuary, rebuilt by an act of courage and faith, still stands watch over the river and the community.

HOMER UNITED METHODIST CHURCH, HOMER, MINNESOTA

81

*J*ust as immigrants from Russia topped their churches with the onion domes that reminded them of home, other settlers also constructed churches that would have looked completely appropriate in their home-lands.

Church of the Redeemer in Cannon Falls, Minnesota, its stonework covered with vines, could have been transported from an English village. Its English roots were reinforced by immigrant clergy such as Thomas Crump, pastor at the turn of the century, who was born and raised in London.

The first time I saw this small Episcopal church in Cannon Falls, rays of the setting sun danced across the ivy-covered exterior, animating the walls of the building. It looked like a ship of souls navigating the currents of life.

CHURCH OF THE REDEEMER, CANNON FALLS, MINNESOTA

83

In the pursuit of their destiny, many people are drawn away from their hometowns. Although they may live and work far far from their childhood homes, they look back and remember their roots and the impact that small churches had on their lives.

A youngster who attended Sunday school and confirmation at Benton United Methodist Church moved to New York and eventually became a millionaire, but he never forgot this tiny community or his boyhood church. He expressed his appreciation with a million dollar bequest which has enabled the congregation to refurbish the church building and the Sunday School wing. Now the church has a new look and a guardian angel as well.

BENTON UNITED METHODIST CHURCH, BENTON, WISCONSIN   85

*W*hen congregations are very small, their members become an extended family for each other. The people of St. Lukes Lutheran Church in Foster, Wisconsin, only twenty-five families strong, connect with each other as one such family of faith. Listen to their reflections.

> *St. Lukes is a heart-warming place. The family of our church is very close.*—LINDA RAUTER

> *It's nice to go to a church where "everyone knows your name."* —JUANITA BUCHHOLZ

> *In the past six or seven years, we have come through fire, flood, and a tornado. Working together, our hope and our faith have brought us through them all.*
> —ALICE GUNDERSON

In these times, everyone could benefit from belonging to such a family.

ST. LUKES LUTHERAN CHURCH, FOSTER, WISCONSIN

*T*ravelers who need shelter from icy winter winds will find that the doors of many rural churches are never locked. In 1981, Bill Aikens, carrying on a tradition of welcoming the stranger, began work on Chapel in the Pines, cutting and trimming, notching and laying logs, using a skill he had learned from his father. He wanted to build a place where people could be alone with God and pray. The hand-hewn log chapel, which nestles in a grove of pine trees near the edge of a winding road, offers an open door, a warm stove, and cozy solitude for weary travelers who have strayed off life's busy highway.

CHAPEL IN THE PINES, ARENA, WISCONSIN

$\mathcal{S}$t. John's Evangelical Lutheran Church in Lake Mills, Wisconsin, is bordered by a four-lane freeway. On the Sunday morning that I attended services there, both song and sermon were accompanied by the hum of steel-belted tires as people hurried to other destinations.

During a midwinter blizzard, when I was returning from the East, visibility was reduced to just a few feet on the interstate, and traffic crawled along very slowly. Blowing winds and snow disoriented me until, through the whiteout, I caught a glimpse of St. John's light ahead, indicating that I was close to home. Like a lighthouse on the outer reach of lands end, it gave me a feeling of safe harbor ahead.

ST. JOHN'S EVANGELICAL LUTHERAN CHURCH, LAKE MILLS, WISCONSIN

If you are curious about the age of a church, consider the height of the trees that surround it. The trees that now tower over many heartland churches were mere saplings when the buildings were erected.

When All Saints Church was constructed in Northfield, Minnesota, small pines were planted in the churchyard. Over the years those trees have grown to rooftop height and now mimic the shape of the steeple.

God has blessed this church with a whole congregation of living steeples. Earth has reached toward heaven, embracing the church, the steeple, and the cross high above. Heaven has touched the earth, embracing this community of faith.

ALL SAINTS CHURCH, NORTHFIELD, MINNESOTA

*T*hroughout the ages, when faced with life-threatening disease, people have turned to God for help. This was certainly true for early settlers, living in harsh conditions, far from medical care.

In 1857, John Endres built a tiny stone chapel, St. Mary of the Oaks, fulfilling a vow he had made in gratitude to Mary, the Mother of God, for protecting the lives of his family during a diptheria epidemic. Aided by his son Peter, John hauled tons of stone to the hilltop overlooking Indian Lake and nestled the chapel among oak and evergreen trees high above the landscape of tilled fields and prairie grasses. Today it still stands witness to God's grace in time of need.

ST. MARY OF THE OAKS CHAPEL, INDIAN LAKE, WISCONSIN

*B*eautifully kept churchyard cemeteries declare the care and respect a community offers to all its members, living and dead. Sadly, this seems less true in large cities.

When I travel to New York, I pass a huge urban graveyard on my way from the airport into the city. It seems to extend for miles—gray, cold, depressing, the occupants crowded together in death as they were in life. The headstones of tiny rural cemeteries look so very different—rather like a group of friends, gathered together in death as they were in life.

Evergreen Hill nestles in a grove of trees above the farm fields of Middleton, Wisconsin, where many of its residents labored throughout their lives. Quiet and serene, it's what a cemetery should be, a peaceful place of rest for those who have completed their work.

EVERGREEN HILL CEMETERY, MIDDLETON, WISCONSIN

*M*y steeple chase concludes in Lanesboro, Minnesota, where the Bethlehem Lutheran and St. Patrick's Catholic steeples stretch toward the sky. I was told by people in the town that one of those churches was built to stand a foot higher than the other, right across the street from it, but I chose to draw them at the same height. In God's eyes, I believe this is more accurate, just as I believe that in God's eyes, a tiny woodland chapel is just as significant as a monumental cathedral.

*H*aving, for the moment, finished this part of my journey, I now hope you will begin your own journey, exploring the heartland for yourself. Whenever you see a steeple in the distance, turn toward it and investigate. The churches you will find are the taproots of our history, our customs, and our patterns of life. Keep an open heart to the humanity and history each church has witnessed and to the homage it pays to our relationship with God.

DIRECTIONS

Use this map and these brief directions as a general guide to the location of each church. For more explicit instructions, contact the church or local visitor centers.

2   Chippewa Mission, Chippewa Valley, WI
    Between Holcombe and Cornell near Brunet Island State Park

5   Cross of Christ Lutheran Church, Red Wing, MN
    Near the intersection of Highway 61 and County 7

7   Our Lady of the Holy Rosary Catholic Church, Grand Portage, MN
    Located on a hill overlooking Grand Portage

9   Simpson Chapel, Dodgeville, WI
    East of Dodgeville near the Military Ridge bike trail

11 Immanuel Lutheran Church, Hay Creek, MN
    24686 Old Church Road, 7 miles south of Red Wing on Highway 58

13 First Presbyterian Church, Pardeeville, WI
    At Highway 22, thirty miles north of Madison on Highway 51

15 Shopiere Congregational Church, Shopiere, WI
    4 miles east of Beloit near the Tiffany Stone Arch Bridge

17 Valley Grove Church, near Nerstrand, MN
    South of Northfield on Highway 246 to County 29, one-half mile north to preservation site on hilltop

19 St. Wenceslaus Island Church, Waterloo, WI
    Off Highway 89 between Lake Mills and Marshall

21 Lakeview Lutheran Chapel, Madison, WI
    5 miles northeast of the capitol on Northport Drive

49 St. John's Lutheran, Mazomanie, WI
    On County Y as it enters Mazomanie from the north

51 Cedar Grove Lutheran Church, near Pickwick, MN
    10 miles south of Winona on Highway 6, turn on County 9

53 Assumption Chapel, Cold Spring, MN
    On Chapel Street in Cold Spring

54 Tripoli Congregational Church, Tripoli, WI
    On the south side of Highway 8 west of Tripoli

57 Christ Church, Old Frontenac, MN
    South of Red Wing 5 miles on Highway 61 to Frontenac exit, then east

59 Hauge Log Church, Perry, WI
    One mile off Highway 78, south of Mt. Horeb on County Z

61 Denzer United Methodist Church, Denzer, WI
    8 miles north on Highway 12 from Prairie de Su c to Highway C

63 Holy Assumption Orthodox Church, Lublin, WI
    West from Medford on Highway 64 to County F, south to Lublin

65 Evangelical Lutheran Church, Mt. Horeb, WI
    20 miles west of Madison off Highway 18/151

67 The Nativity of the Blessed Virgin Mary Church, St. Mary's, WI
    7 miles from Cashton on County U near Norwalk

69 St. Peter's Lutheran Church, Shennington, WI
    North of Tomah on Highway 21, west of Wyeville

71 Isherwood's Cradle, near Stevens Point, WI
    Hwy 10 east of Plover to Isherwood Road, turn south to Birch Road, west
    1 mile. Cradle is located at the edge of the road in a grove of trees.

73 Holy Redeemer Catholic Church, Perry, WI
    Located in the town of Perry, 7 miles south of Mt. Horeb off Highway 78

74 East Wiota Lutheran Church, South Wayne, WI
8 miles southwest of Argyle on Hwy 78

77 St. Mary's Orthodox Church, Cornucopia, WI
West of Bayfield along Highway 13 near Lake Superior

79 Vasa Church, Vasa, MN
Off County 19, 10 miles from Red Wing

81 Homer United Methodist Church, Homer, MN
5 miles south of Winona off Highway 14/61 in Homer

83 Church of the Redeemer, Cannon Falls, MN
Highway 52 to Highway 19, at the corner of Highway 19 and 4th Street

85 Benton United Methodist Church, Benton, WI
On the north side of Highway 11 in Benton

87 St. Luke's Lutheran Church, Foster, WI
Halfway between Osseo and Eau Claire on Interstate 94 at Park Avenue
and Coon Street

89 Chapel in the Pines, Arena, WI
20 miles west of Madison on Highway 14

91 St. John's Evangelical Lutheran Church, Lake Mills, WI
Highway B out of Lake Mills, turn right on Newville Road, the steeple can
be seen from the top of the hill

93 All Saints Church, Northfield, MN
In Northfield on the corner of 5th and Washington Street

95 St. Mary of the Oaks, Indian Lake, WI
Near Highway 19, west of Highway 12, located in a county park

97 Evergreen Hill, Middleton, WI
West of Middleton just off Airport Road

99 Bethlehem Lutheran Church, St. Patrick's Catholic Church, Lanesboro, MN
Highway 16 to Lanesboro, can be seen on a hill in town